THE DATA CENTER FIRE SAFETY HANDBOOK: PREVENTION, PREPAREDNESS, AND RECOVERY

PREFACE

The hum of servers, the flicker of LEDs, the vast repository of our digital lives – data centers are the throbbing hearts of our connected world. They store our memories, fuel our businesses, and connect us across continents. Yet, a silent threat lurks within these technological marvels: fire.

This book isn't just about data center fires; it's about **resilience**: the ability to withstand, adapt, and emerge stronger in the face of adversity. It's about understanding the complexities of fire hazards, exploring the devastating consequences of fire incidents, and illuminating the pathways to prevention, preparedness, and recovery.

Why this book matters:

- **The stakes are high.** Data loss, business disruption, and even human lives are on the line in a data center fire.
- **Knowledge is power.** By understanding the risks and mitigation strategies, stakeholders can make informed decisions and protect their critical infrastructure.
- **Prevention is key.** A proactive approach towards fire safety minimizes damage and ensures business continuity.
- **Technology is our ally.** Innovative solutions like advanced detection systems and training simulations are revolutionizing fire safety practices.
- **Human vigilance is irreplaceable.** Skilled personnel, clear communication protocols, and a culture of safety are the foundations of effective fire response.

What you'll find:

- **Comprehensive overview:** Delve into the different types of fire hazards, suppression systems, and emergency response protocols.
- **Real-world insights:** Case studies and expert opinions illustrate the practical application of fire safety principles.
- **Future-focused perspective:** Explore cutting-edge technologies and trends shaping the future of data center fire safety.
- **Actionable knowledge:** Each chapter concludes with practical takeaways and resources for implementation.

This book is for everyone invested in the world of data centers: **IT professionals, facility managers, security personnel, executives, and even individuals concerned about the security of their digital data.** By fostering a shared understanding of fire safety challenges and solutions, we can collectively build a more resilient digital future.

Remember, fire safety is not a destination, but a continuous journey. Let's embark on this journey together, embracing the knowledge and proactive measures within these pages to ensure our data centers, and the invaluable information they hold, remain safe from the flames.

Ready to face the inferno? Turn the page and begin your journey.

ABOUT THE AUTHOR:

Charles Nehme is an Electro- Mechanical Engineer with 32 Years of international experience, data centers inclusive. Profile https://bit.ly/m/HVAC

Extinguishing Agent Bottles

CHAPTER 1: INFERNO IN THE MACHINE: FIRE HAZARDS IN DATA CENTERS

The hum of countless servers, the steady blink of LED lights, the controlled chill of the air—a data center is a symphony of controlled chaos, housing the lifeblood of our digital world. But within this carefully-tuned environment lurks a constant threat: fire. A single spark, a malfunctioning cooling system, a misplaced cigarette—any of these seemingly minor events can erupt into an inferno, unleashing devastation on both physical infrastructure and the irreplaceable data it stores.

This chapter delves into the hidden dangers lurking within data centers, exploring the various fire hazards that threaten their existence. We'll examine the common culprits, from electrical faults and overheating equipment to flammable materials and human error. Each section will detail the specific risks, providing real-world examples and statistics to illustrate their potential impact.

Electrical Mayhem: A Conductor of Catastrophe

Data centers are powered by a complex web of electrical wiring and components. While vital for operation, this very dependence creates a multitude of fire hazards. Faulty wiring, overloaded circuits, and malfunctioning electrical equipment can all generate heat and sparks, igniting combustible materials nearby. Additionally, power surges and lightning strikes pose significant threats, potentially causing widespread damage and system failures.

Case Study: In 2017, a data center fire in London, England, was traced back to an electrical fault in a UPS system. The fire caused extensive damage and disrupted services for several major companies, highlighting the critical need for proper electrical maintenance and safety protocols.

The Silent Enemy: Overheating Equipment

The relentless processing power of servers generates significant heat, and proper cooling is paramount to prevent overheating. However, malfunctions in cooling systems, clogged air filters, and inadequate airflow can all lead to equipment reaching critical temperatures, creating a perfect recipe for combustion. Additionally, dust buildup on servers and other components can act as fuel, further exacerbating the risk.

Did You Know? A study by Uptime Institute revealed that cooling system failures are the leading cause of data center outages, with a significant portion linked to fire incidents.

Flammable Foes: Hidden Dangers in Plain Sight

While data centers strive for efficiency, some elements simply can't be eliminated. Cables, storage media, and even certain cleaning products often contain flammable materials. Improper storage, inadequate fire barriers, and accidental spills can all create dangerous situations. Additionally, construction materials and other organic matter within the facility can contribute to the spread of fire once ignited.

Fact: A 2020 report by the National Fire Protection Association (NFPA) identified combustible storage as a major factor in over 60% of data center fire incidents.

The Human Factor: When Mistakes Have Consequences

No matter how advanced the technology, data centers ultimately rely on human input and intervention. Unfortunately, human error can be a significant contributor to fire hazards. Unintentional misuse of equipment, neglecting safety protocols, and improper disposal of flammable materials can all have disastrous consequences.

Remember: Regular training and awareness programs are crucial in minimizing human error and fostering a culture of safety within the data center workforce.

By understanding these diverse fire hazards, data center operators, designers, and staff can take proactive steps to mitigate risks and prevent tragedy. The next chapter will delve into the devastating consequences of fire in data centers, highlighting the critical need for comprehensive fire protection strategies.

CHAPTER 2: ASHES OF PROGRESS: THE IMPACT OF FIRE ON DATA CENTERS

A data center fire is not just a physical inferno; it's a digital apocalypse. Beyond the charred equipment and melted cables lies a deeper devastation: the potential loss of irreplaceable data, crippling downtime, and severe consequences for businesses and individuals alike. This chapter explores the multifaceted impact of fire on data centers, illuminating the true cost of this modern-day disaster.

The Tangible Toll: Damage to Equipment and Infrastructure

The immediate and most visible consequence of a fire is physical damage. Sensitive servers, storage devices, and intricate network infrastructure are all highly vulnerable to heat, smoke, and water used for extinguishing the flames. Even minor fires can render equipment inoperable, requiring costly replacements and lengthy repair processes.

Case Study: The 2021 OVHcloud fire in Strasbourg, France, destroyed an entire data center, affecting over 65,000 customers and resulting in an estimated loss of €105 million. This incident starkly illustrates the potential financial devastation caused by data center fires.

The Intangible Loss: Data Disintegration and Disruption

Data is the lifeblood of the digital age, and its loss can be catastrophic. While backups are crucial, fire can often compromise them too, especially if located within the same facility. Businesses reliant on cloud platforms may also face data loss if stored in affected servers. This translates to lost financial records, customer information, intellectual property, and even personal memories, creating an intangible yet undeniable impact.

Did You Know? A study by Ponemon Institute estimated the average cost of a data breach at $4.24 million, highlighting the financial implications of compromised data. Data loss from a fire can have similar, if not more severe, consequences.

The Ripple Effect: Business Interruption and Reputational Damage

For many businesses, data centers are the central nervous system. A fire-induced outage can cripple operations, causing lost revenue, productivity, and customer trust. The impact can cascade across industries, affecting everything from financial transactions to healthcare services. In an ever-connected world, even short outages can have significant repercussions.

Fact: A recent Uptime Institute survey revealed that the average cost of a single hour of data center downtime is $8,850, emphasizing the critical need for business continuity planning.

The Human Cost: Safety Risks and Public Impact

Beyond the financial and operational aspects, data center fires also pose a significant threat to human safety. Firefighters battling the blaze face risks from hazardous materials, toxic fumes, and structural collapse. Additionally, depending on the data center's location, nearby communities may be exposed to smoke and potential environmental hazards.

Remember: Comprehensive safety protocols and emergency response plans are essential to protecting the lives of both data center personnel and the surrounding community.

By understanding the multi-faceted impact of fire on data centers, stakeholders can prioritize prevention strategies, invest in robust fire protection systems, and implement effective disaster recovery plans. The next chapter will explore these proactive measures, empowering data center operators to safeguard their critical infrastructure and the invaluable data it holds.

CHAPTER 3: GUARDIAN ANGELS WITH HOSES: FIRE PROTECTION SYSTEMS IN DATA CENTERS

Standing vigilant against the ever-present threat of fire, a network of sophisticated systems forms the first line of defense in data centers. This chapter delves into the various fire protection solutions available, empowering stakeholders to choose the right safeguards for their specific needs.

Smoke Signals: Early Detection is Key

The sooner a fire is detected, the faster it can be contained and extinguished. Data centers utilize a range of detection systems, including:

Heat detectors: Respond to rapid temperature increases.

Smoke detectors: Identify smoke particles, often using advanced ionization or laser technology.

Aspirating smoke detection (ASD): Actively draws air samples, offering high sensitivity and early detection.

Early detection allows for immediate action, minimizing damage and potential data loss.

Dousing the Flames: Suppression Systems Take Action

Once a fire is detected, various suppression systems come into play:

Water-based systems: Traditional sprinkler systems are widely used, but pre-action and mist versions minimize water damage risks.

Gas-based systems: Clean agents like FM-200 and Novec 1230 extinguish fire by displacing oxygen, leaving minimal residue.

Chemical agent systems: Halon is being phased out due to environmental concerns, replaced by newer options like Inergen.

Choosing the right system depends on factors like data sensitivity, personnel safety, and environmental impact.

Beyond the System: Building and Design Considerations

Building design and construction play a crucial role in fire protection:

Fire-resistant materials: Walls, floors, and ceilings should be constructed with fire-resistant materials like concrete or fire-treated wood.

Compartmentalization: Dividing the data center into smaller fire zones prevents widespread fire spread.

Raised floors: These create a space for cable management and can facilitate fire suppression system deployment.

Cable management: Proper cable routing and fire-resistant enclosures minimize fuel sources and impede fire spread.

Integrating these design features creates a physical barrier against fire, complementing active suppression systems.

Constant Vigilance: Operational Procedures and Training

Even the most advanced systems require human intervention for maximum effectiveness. Here's how operational procedures and training contribute:

Hot work permits: Ensure proper safety measures are followed during activities like welding or soldering.

Housekeeping: Regular cleaning prevents flammable material buildup, reducing fire hazards.

Equipment maintenance: Scheduled maintenance minimizes equipment malfunctions that could spark fires.

Staff training: Regular training equips personnel with fire safety knowledge and response procedures.

By combining active systems with passive design features and proactive operational practices, data centers can create a multi-layered defense against fire and its devastating consequences.

The next chapter will explore the importance of emergency planning and post-fire recovery, ensuring data centers are prepared to weather even the most unforeseen events.

CHAPTER 4: FROM INFERNO TO PHOENIX: BUILDING A RESILIENT DATA CENTER

A fire may erupt, systems may fail, but a data center's story doesn't end there. This chapter focuses on the crucial aspects of emergency planning and post-fire recovery, empowering data centers to rise from the ashes and ensure business continuity.

Section 1: The Crucial Plan: Fire Emergency Response

A well-defined fire emergency plan is the cornerstone of effective response. This section outlines key elements:

Evacuation procedures: Clearly defined evacuation routes and procedures ensure personnel safety during a fire event.

Firefighter access and operations: Facilitate firefighter access with clear signage, designated entry points, and floor plans.

Data recovery plan: Establish a comprehensive data recovery plan, including backups, offsite storage, and restoration procedures.

By regularly testing and updating the plan, data centers can ensure a coordinated and effective response in the face of fire.

Section 2: Rising from the Ashes: Post-Fire Recovery

Even after the flames are extinguished, the journey to recovery is far from over. This section explores key steps:

Damage assessment: Evaluate the extent of damage to equipment, infrastructure, and data.

Equipment restoration: Repair or replace damaged equipment, prioritizing critical systems for business continuity.

Data recovery: Implement the data recovery plan, restoring lost or corrupted data from backups.

Business continuity: Implement contingency plans to minimize downtime and ensure business operations resume as quickly as possible.

A well-executed post-fire recovery plan minimizes disruption and ensures a smooth transition back to normal operations.

Conclusion

By investing in fire protection systems, implementing robust operational procedures, and building a comprehensive emergency response and recovery plan, data centers can build resilience against fire and emerge stronger from any challenge. Remember, fire safety is not a one-time effort; it's an ongoing commitment that safeguards our critical digital infrastructure and the invaluable data it holds.

CHAPTER 5: BEYOND THE SPARK: EMBRACING CONTINUOUS IMPROVEMENT IN FIRE SAFETY

Fire safety in data centers is not a static destination, but an ongoing journey of learning, adaptation, and improvement. This chapter explores emerging technologies, continuous risk assessment, and fostering a culture of safety to keep data centers protected in an ever-evolving landscape.

Embracing Innovation: The Future of Fire Protection

Technology plays a crucial role in advancing fire safety, offering exciting possibilities:

Advanced detection systems: Utilizing artificial intelligence and machine learning for pre-emptive fire prediction and anomaly detection.

Smart suppression systems: Systems that adapt to real-time fire dynamics, using targeted suppression methods for increased efficiency and minimal damage.

Virtual reality training: Immersive training simulations for personnel to hone their fire response skills in a safe and controlled environment.

By staying informed about and implementing these advancements, data centers can stay ahead of the curve and mitigate emerging fire risks.

The Vigilant Eye: Continuous Risk Assessment

Complacency is the enemy of progress. Regular risk assessments are crucial for identifying vulnerabilities and adapting safety measures:

Conduct regular fire hazards analysis: Evaluate new equipment, processes, and environmental factors that may introduce new risks.

Test and update fire protection systems: Ensure all systems are functioning optimally and compliant with current regulations.

Perform fire drills and simulations: Practice emergency response procedures to identify areas for improvement and ensure personnel preparedness.

Continuous risk assessment allows data centers to proactively address evolving threats and maintain a robust safety posture.

Cultivating a Culture of Safety: Empowering Individuals

Ultimately, fire safety hinges on human behavior. Fostering

a culture of safety empowers individuals to become active participants in fire prevention and response:

Invest in employee training: Provide comprehensive fire safety training, including fire extinguisher use, evacuation procedures, and hazard identification.

Empower staff to report concerns: Encourage open communication about potential fire hazards and encourage a culture of safety first.

Recognize and reward safety-conscious behavior: Promote safe practices and positive safety behaviors through recognition programs.

By empowering individuals and fostering a safety-conscious culture, data centers can create an environment where responsible actions become second nature.

In conclusion, fire safety in data centers is not merely a checklist of systems and procedures, but a dynamic and continuous effort. By embracing emerging technologies, conducting regular risk assessments, and cultivating a culture of safety, data centers can ensure their critical infrastructure remains protected against the ever-present threat of fire, safeguarding the invaluable data entrusted to them.

CHAPTER 6: FACING THE INFERNO: FIRE EMERGENCY PLAN IN ACTION

A fire alarm echoes through the data center, jolting everyone from their tasks. Smoke seeps through vents, triggering the pre-programmed response from fire protection systems. In this adrenaline-charged moment, a well-rehearsed fire emergency plan becomes the lifeline for personnel, equipment, and irreplaceable data.

This chapter delves into the heart of a fire emergency, guiding you through the crucial steps of executing a comprehensive fire response plan and ensuring the safety of people, data, and infrastructure.

Section 1: Evacuation: Every Second Counts

Immediate action: Upon hearing the alarm, personnel must immediately follow designated evacuation routes, avoiding elevators and using designated stairwells.

Accountability: Floor wardens ensure everyone evacuates and

conducts headcount at designated assembly points outside the building.

Communication: Designated personnel contact emergency services, providing crucial information about the fire location and potential hazards.

Remember, speed and order are paramount during evacuation. Regular drills ensure everyone knows their roles and can act swiftly.

Section 2: Battling the Blaze: Supporting Firefighters

Facilitating access: Entry points and routes for firefighters are clearly marked and unobstructed. Floor plans and hazard information are readily available.

Power and utilities: Designated personnel shut down non-critical systems and utilities to minimize risks and potential explosions.

Data center isolation: If possible, fire doors and compartmentalization measures are activated to contain the fire and protect other areas.

Cooperation with firefighters is crucial. Clear communication and understanding of the facility's layout ensure their efforts are optimized for maximum effectiveness.

Section 3: Data in Peril: Safeguarding the Digital Lifeline

Data center shutdown: If safe, trained personnel attempt to shut down critical servers and equipment in a controlled manner to minimize data loss.

Activation of backups: Backup systems are activated automatically or manually to ensure data redundancy and minimize data loss.

Offsite data protection: If fire threatens to engulf the entire facility, protocols for accessing and restoring data from offsite backups are initiated.

Protecting data throughout the fire event is a core priority. Pre-established backup procedures and offsite storage ensure business continuity and minimize data loss.

Section 4: Recovery and Aftermath: Picking Up the Pieces

Damage assessment: Once the fire is extinguished, fire marshals and technical teams assess the damage to equipment, infrastructure, and data.

Data recovery: The data recovery plan is implemented, utilizing backups and established procedures to restore lost or corrupted data.

Equipment restoration: Damaged equipment is repaired or replaced, prioritizing critical systems to ensure business continuity.

Post-incident analysis: A thorough review of the fire event and response identifies areas for improvement in the emergency plan and overall safety protocols.

The journey doesn't end with the fire being extinguished. A comprehensive recovery plan ensures efficient repair, data restoration, and continuous learning to strengthen future preparedness.

By having a well-defined and regularly practiced fire emergency plan, data centers can navigate even the most challenging fire events with increased efficiency, minimizing damage, ensuring personal safety, and safeguarding the precious data entrusted to them. Remember, fire safety is a shared responsibility, and every individual plays a crucial role in preventing, responding to, and recovering from fire emergencies.

CHAPTER 7: TESTING THE WATERS: ADVANCED FIRE DRILLS AND SIMULATIONS IN DATA CENTERS

While comprehensive fire emergency plans and regular training are crucial, true preparedness requires testing beyond paper and theory. This chapter dives into the increasingly sophisticated world of advanced fire drills and simulations, empowering data centers to refine their response and ensure their teams are ready to face the unexpected.

Beyond the Basics: Expanding the Drill Repertoire

Traditional fire drills typically focus on evacuation procedures. While essential, the scope needs to widen to account for the complexities of data center environments. Consider these advanced drill types:

Real-time response drills: Introduce unexpected scenarios during drills, mimicking real-fire situations and testing decision-making skills under pressure.

Equipment handling drills: Train personnel on operating fire extinguishers and using other fire suppression equipment safely and effectively.

Data center shutdown drills: Practice controlled shutdown procedures for critical servers and other equipment to minimize data loss during an actual fire.

Multi-agency coordination drills: Simulate collaboration with firefighters and other emergency responders, ensuring seamless cooperation and communication during a real event.

By diversifying training scenarios, data centers can assess and strengthen their team's response capabilities across various situations.

Embracing Technology: The Power of Simulation

Traditional drills offer valuable experience, but technology can take it further. Consider these advanced simulation tools:

Virtual reality (VR) simulations: Immerse personnel in realistic fire scenarios within a controlled VR environment, providing a safe and engaging training experience.

Tabletop exercises: Gather key stakeholders to discuss hypothetical fire scenarios, strategize responses, and identify potential vulnerabilities.

Computer-aided simulations: Simulate fire spread and smoke

movement within the data center layout, helping optimize response strategies and resource allocation.

These tools provide a safe and controlled space to test plans, identify weak points, and practice complex procedures, ensuring a more comprehensive and nuanced response in a real-fire situation.

Measuring Success: Beyond Smoke and Mirrors

Effective fire drills and simulations require proper evaluation and feedback mechanisms. Here's how:

Debriefing and analysis: After each drill, conduct thorough debriefings with participants, identifying strengths, weaknesses, and areas for improvement.

Metrics and performance tracking: Use measurable metrics to track progress and assess the effectiveness of drills and training programs.

Regular review and updates: Regularly review fire emergency plans and training procedures based on feedback and lessons learned from drills and simulations.

By actively measuring, analyzing, and adapting, data centers can ensure their drills and simulations translate into tangible improvements in preparedness and response capabilities.

The Investment in Safety: Reaping the Rewards

Advanced fire drills and simulations may seem like an additional expense, but the benefits outweigh the costs:

Reduced risks and improved safety: Enhanced preparedness translates to faster and more effective response, minimizing damage and ensuring personnel safety.

Minimized data loss: Practicing data center shutdown procedures and having robust backup systems in place can significantly reduce data loss during a fire event.

Increased business continuity: Efficient incident response and recovery lead to less downtime and faster resumption of critical operations.

Reduced insurance premiums: Demonstrating a strong commitment to fire safety can lead to lower insurance costs for data centers.

Investing in advanced fire drills and simulations is an investment in peace of mind, safety, and ultimately, the business's resilience and ability to weather unforeseen challenges.

This chapter concludes by emphasizing the importance of continuously testing and refining fire response strategies through advanced drills and simulations. By embracing technology, measuring success, and recognizing the tangible benefits, data centers can build a culture of preparedness, ensuring they are truly ready to face the flames and safeguard their critical infrastructure and invaluable data.

CHAPTER 8: LOOKING AHEAD: FUTURE TRENDS IN DATA CENTER FIRE SAFETY

While significant strides have been made in data center fire safety, the future holds even more advancements, driven by technology, sustainability, and a growing focus on proactive risk management. This chapter explores some key trends shaping the future of fire protection in data centers.

The Rise of Predictive Analytics: Leveraging artificial intelligence and machine learning algorithms, data centers will increasingly utilize predictive analytics to anticipate potential fire hazards. By analyzing temperature fluctuations, equipment performance data, and even weather patterns, systems can identify anomalies and predict fire risks before they escalate.

Smarter Suppression Systems: Fire suppression systems will evolve beyond blanket approaches, featuring adaptive technology that adjusts suppression methods based on the specific characteristics of the fire. Imagine systems using drones for targeted suppression, minimizing water damage and environmental impact.

Focus on Sustainability: Sustainable fire suppression solutions will gain traction, with the use of eco-friendly alternatives like inert gas mixtures and water mist systems becoming more widespread. This will not only benefit the environment but also address concerns about the potential harm posed by traditional chemical agents.

Cybersecurity Convergence: As data centers become increasingly interconnected, the lines between physical and cybersecurity threats will blur. Fire safety systems will need to integrate with cybersecurity measures to detect and prevent malicious attacks that could trigger fires.

Collaborative Risk Management: Data centers will move towards collaborative risk management, sharing threat intelligence and best practices with industry peers and emergency responders. This collective approach will foster continuous improvement and proactive risk mitigation strategies.

Standardized Regulations: Efforts towards standardized fire safety regulations for data centers across different regions will likely gain momentum. This will ensure consistent safety standards and facilitate knowledge sharing and technology adoption globally.

The Human Factor Remains Key: Despite technological advancements, the human element will remain central to effective fire safety. Ongoing training, clear communication protocols, and a culture of safety awareness will be critical in ensuring quick and decisive response during fire emergencies.

Beyond these specific trends, the future of data center fire safety is likely to be characterized by ongoing innovation, continuous learning, and a collaborative approach to risk management. By embracing these trends and prioritizing proactive prevention, data centers can ensure the security of their critical infrastructure and protect the valuable data entrusted to them in a sustainable and responsible manner.

This concluding chapter emphasizes the dynamic nature of data center fire safety. As technology evolves and threats change, continuous adaptation, knowledge sharing, and a commitment to responsible practices will be key to shaping a safe and secure future for our digital infrastructure.

Duct Fire Damper (data centers usually have 2 hours fire wall ratings) The damper shall withstand this.

CONCLUSION: A SYMPHONY OF RESILIENCE

Data centers, the humming hearts of our digital world, pulsate with immense potential and responsibility. They safeguard our memories, fuel our businesses, and connect us globally. Yet, this vital infrastructure faces a constant threat: fire.

This book has delved into the complexities of fire hazards in data centers, explored the devastating consequences of fire incidents, and illuminated the various pathways to prevention, preparedness, and recovery. From fire detection systems and suppression strategies to robust emergency plans and advanced training simulations, each chapter has emphasized the multi-layered approach required to safeguard these critical facilities.

Remember, fire safety in data centers is not a static set of procedures; it's a dynamic journey of continuous learning and improvement. By embracing emerging technologies, conducting regular risk assessments, and fostering a culture of safety, data centers can build resilience against fire and emerge stronger from any challenge.

As we look to the future, exciting advancements like predictive analytics, smarter suppression systems, and collaborative risk management promise to enhance fire safety even further. However, amidst these technological leaps, remember the enduring importance of the human element. Skilled personnel, clear communication protocols, and a vigilant safety culture will always be the bedrock of effective fire prevention and response.

Ultimately, by prioritizing fire safety, data centers not only protect their infrastructure and data, but also ensure the uninterrupted flow of the digital lifeblood that powers our modern world. Remember, a spark can become a blaze, but through awareness, preparation, and proactive measures, we can ensure that the symphony of data centers continues to play, resilient and secure, for generations to come.

This concludes the book "Firefighting in Data Centers." Remember, the fight for fire safety is never truly over. Let us all be active participants in safeguarding our critical infrastructure and the irreplaceable data it holds.

ADDITIONAL RESOURCES:

National Fire Protection Association (NFPA): https://www.nfpa.org/en

Uptime Institute: https://uptimeinstitute.com/

The Open Group: https://www.opengroup.org/

GLOSSARY

Glossary for Firefighting in Data Centers

Aspirating smoke detection (ASD): A system that actively draws air samples for early fire detection.

Automatic Fire Detection and Alarm System: System that automatically detects and alerts occupants of a fire.

Cable management: Proper organization and protection of cables to minimize fire hazards.

Clean agent systems: Gas-based suppression systems that use clean agents like FM-200 or Novec 1230 to extinguish fire.

Compartmentalization: Dividing the data center into smaller fire zones to prevent widespread fire spread.

Cooling system failures: A leading cause of data center outages, some linked to fire incidents.

Data backup: Copies of data stored offsite or in a separate location for recovery in case of primary data loss.

Data center shutdown: Controlled shutdown of critical servers and equipment to minimize data loss during a fire.

Data loss: The permanent or unrecoverable deletion of data, often occurring as a result of fire damage.

Data recovery plan: A plan outlining procedures for recovering lost or corrupted data after a fire event.

Electrical faults: Malfunctions in electrical wiring or components that can generate heat and sparks, igniting fires.

Evacuation procedures: Clearly defined routes and procedures for personnel to safely evacuate the data center during a fire.

Fire emergency plan: A comprehensive plan outlining actions to be taken in case of a fire, including evacuation, response measures, and data recovery.

Fire hazards: Potential sources of fire within a data center, including electrical faults, overheating equipment, flammable materials, and human error.

Fire risk assessment: Evaluation of potential fire hazards and vulnerabilities in a data center.

Fire suppression systems: Systems designed to extinguish or control a fire, including water-based, gas-based, and clean agent systems.

Firefighter access and operations: Procedures for facilitating firefighter access to the data center and ensuring their safety during fire response.

Flammable materials: Materials that easily ignite and contribute to the spread of fire.

Halon: A gas-based fire suppressant being phased out due to environmental concerns.

Hot work permits: Permits required for activities that generate heat or sparks, such as welding or soldering.

Human error: Unintentional actions or mistakes that can contribute to fire hazards.

Overheating equipment: Servers and other equipment generating excessive heat, creating a fire risk.

Post-fire recovery: The process of restoring data center operations and equipment after a fire event.

Power surges: Sudden increases in voltage that can damage equipment and potentially spark fires.

Raised floors: A space beneath the data center floor used for cable management and facilitating fire suppression system deployment.

Smoke detectors: Detect smoke particles to identify fire early.

Staff training: Regularly training personnel on fire safety procedures and response protocols.

Water-based systems: Traditional sprinkler systems with various advancements like pre-action and mist versions.

Additional Terms:

Business continuity: Minimizing downtime and ensuring business operations resume quickly after a fire.

Fire resistant materials: Materials that resist fire for a specific period.

Heat detectors: Respond to rapid temperature increases.

NFPA: National Fire Protection Association, a leading source for fire safety standards and information.

Uptime Institute: An organization focused on improving the reliability and efficiency of data centers.

www.ingramcontent.com/pod-product-compliance
Lightning Source LLC
Chambersburg PA
CBHW061057050326
40690CB00012B/2664